Usborne

First Sticker Book
Dinosaurs

Illustrated by Jordan Wray

Words by Hannah Watson

Designed by Keith Newell

Contents

With expert advice from Ed Drewitt

You'll find all the stickers at the back of the book.

Munching leaves

Stick on some more long-necked Diplodocuses and hungry Stegosauruses grazing on plants and trees. Plant-eaters like these are called herbivores.

Stegosaurus

Hatching eggs

This Maiasaura is guarding her nest from Bambiraptors who are waiting to pounce. Maiasaura means 'good mother lizard'. Stick on some more parents and some little babies who have already hatched.

Maiasaura

T-rex attack!

Some scientists now think that the Tyrannosaurus rex had feathers. This fierce T-rex has spotted a Triceratops for lunch! Stick on lots more dinosaurs running away.

T-rex

In a swamp

Edmontosauruses lived in warm, tropical swamps. Stick on some more dinosaurs, and some bright flowers. Fill the water with turtles and fish.

Lepisosteus

Under the sea

Ichthyosaurs and plesiosaurs lived in the ocean, along with spiral-shaped ammonites and lots of prehistoric fish. Add them all to this tropical scene.

Ichthyosaurus
Plesiosaurus

In the air

The wings of the enormous Quetzalcoatlus were as wide as a small plane. Fill the sky with these amazing flying creatures and add another nest of eggs to the clifftop.

By the coast

Scelidosauruses roam this rocky coastline looking for plants to eat, while Dimorphodons fly overhead. Add more of these to the picture and fill the water with sea creatures.

Dimorphodon
Scelidosaurus

More dinosaurs

Find all of the dinosaur stickers to match these shapes and labels. How many do you recognize?

Munching leaves pages 2–3

Hatching eggs pages 4–5

T-rex attack! pages 6–7

In a swamp pages 8–9

Under the sea pages 10–11

In the air pages 12–13

By the coast pages 14–15

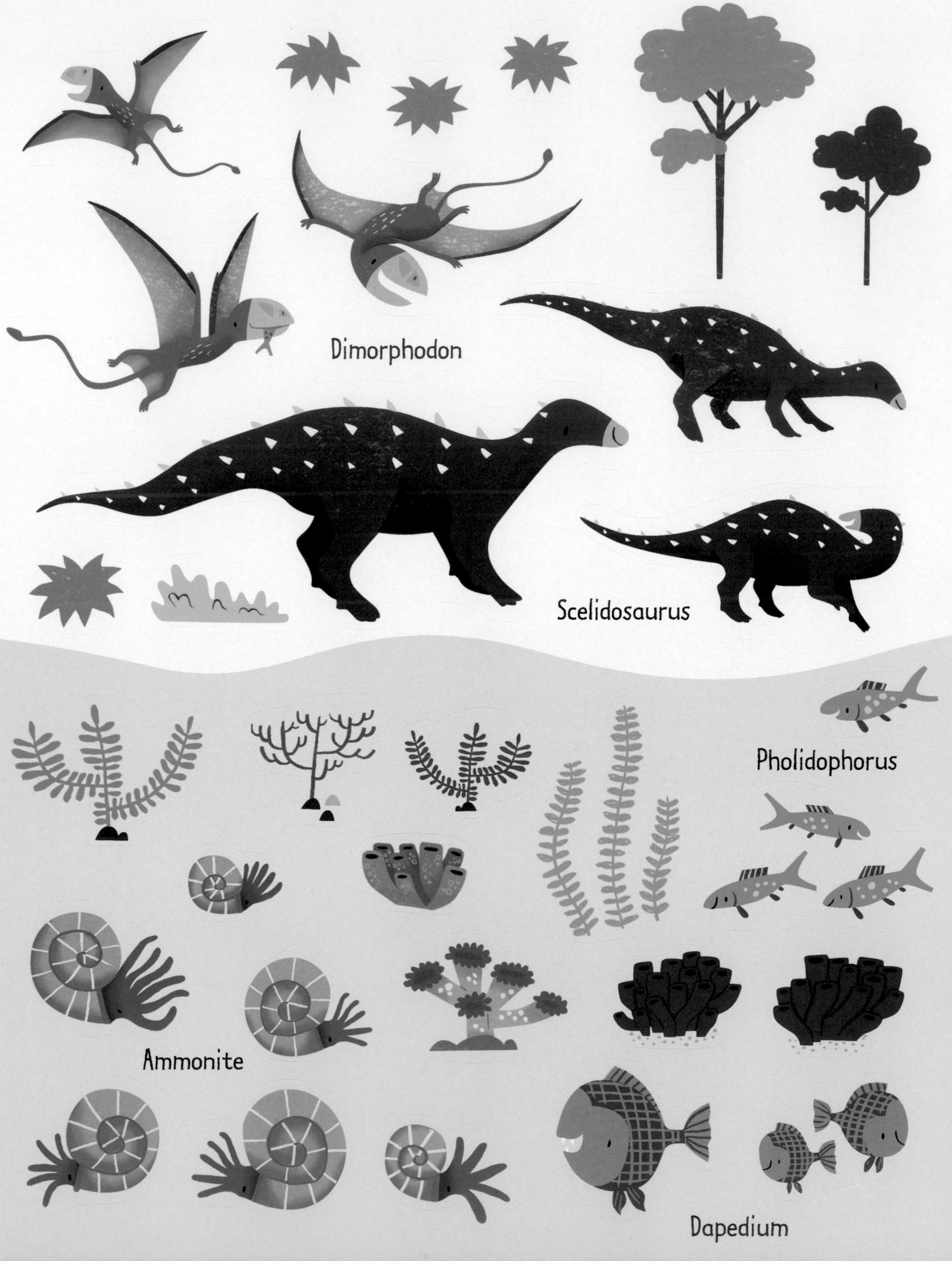

More dinosaurs page 16

Allosaurus

Brachiosaurus

Ankylosaurus

Brontosaurus

Iguanodon

Spinosaurus

Eoraptor

Velociraptor

You can use these stickers anywhere in the book.